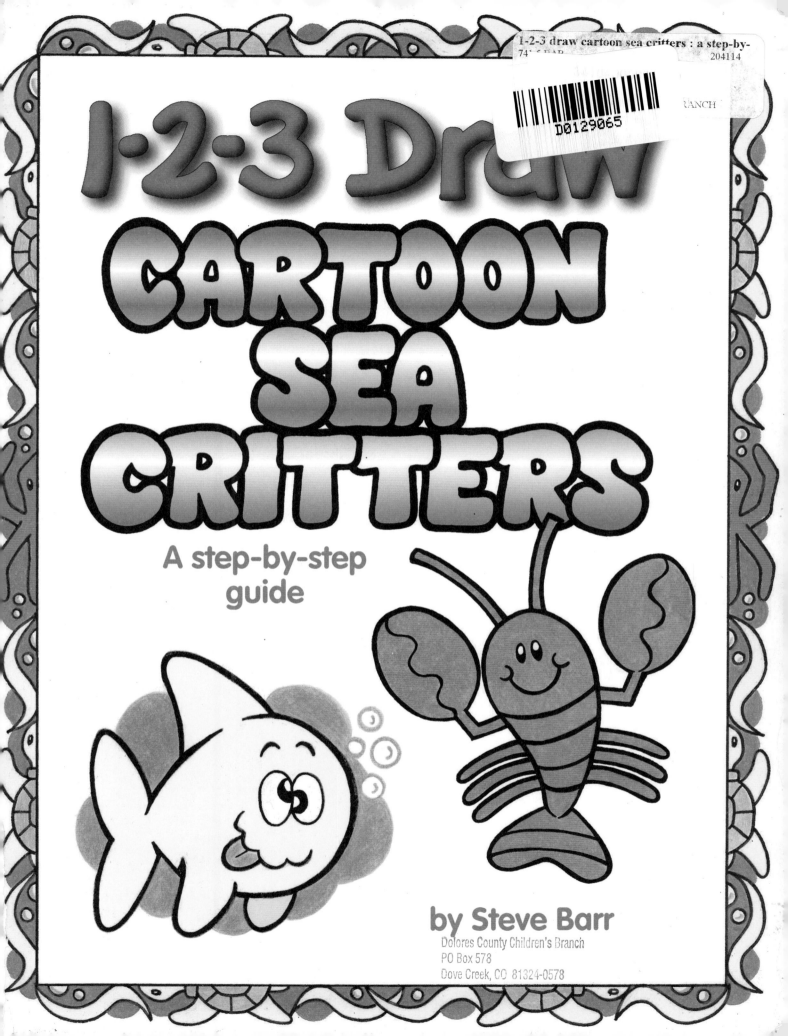

1-2-3 Draw

CARTOON SEA CRITTERS

A step-by-step guide

by Steve Barr

This book is dedicated
to Doug and Susan for
all of their help,
encouragement,
cheerful advice and
assistance.

Library of Congress Cataloging-in-Publication Data

Barr, Steve, 1958-
   1-2-3 draw cartoon sea critters : a step-by-step guide / by Steve
Barr.
     p. cm.
   ISBN 0-939217-72-4 (pbk. : alk. paper)
1. Marine animals--Caricatures and cartoons--Juvenile literature. 2.
Cartooning--Technique--Juvenile literature. [1. Marine animals in art.
2. Cartooning--Technique.] I. Title: One-two-three draw cartoon sea
critters. II. Title.
   NC1764.8.M37 B37 2003
   741.5--dc21   2003001217

Distributed to the trade and art
markets in North America by

NORTH LIGHT BOOKS,
an imprint of F&W Publications, Inc.
4700 East Galbraith Road
Cincinnati, OH 45236

(800) 289-0963

Contents

Before you begin...
Stop! Look! Listen!

You will need:

1. a sharpened pencil
2. paper
3. an eraser
4. a pencil sharpener
5. colored pencils, markers or crayons
6. a comfortable place to sit and draw
7. a good light source

NO RULES!

This book is designed to teach you the basics of cartoon drawing. There are no rules about cartooning! You can use any shapes you want to make a cartoon picture. The fish on this page changes dramatically just by changing the shape of the tail and dorsal fin.

Sketch, doodle, play!

If the instructions tell you to use an oval to draw something and you want to use a square, draw a square. Try out different shapes to see what you can create. Explore and experiment as you go through this book. Change the drawings in this book to make them your very own. If your new drawing makes you giggle, you are doing it right!

Cartooning tips:

1 Draw lightly at first – SKETCH, so you can erase extra lines easily.

2 Practice, practice, practice!

3 Have fun cartooning!

Basic Shapes and Lines

Here are the basic shapes and lines you will use to draw cartoon sea critters:

Oval

Circle

Rectangle

Square

Straight lines

Squiggly lines

Curved lines

Rounded wave

Sharp wave

Valentines

Manta ray

Let's begin by using some of the basic shapes and lines to draw a manta ray.

1 Sketch an oval for the body. Draw a sharp wave shape on each side, for fins.

2 Draw two curved lines to begin the tail. Add a valentine shape to the end, for the tail tip.

3 Sketch a curved line for the mouth. Draw ovals for eyes. Darken part of each eye.

4 LOOK at the final drawing! Erase extra sketch lines. Darken the final lines. Add color.

Nice job!

Manta ray (side view)

A ray is a type of fish with a flat body; large winglike fins; and a small, whiplike tail. Let's draw a side view of a manta ray, using simple shapes and lines.

1 Sketch a slightly flattened oval for the body.

2 Draw two curved lines for the tail. Add a valentine shape for the tail tip.

3 Draw two sharp wave shapes, connecting to the body, for the fins.

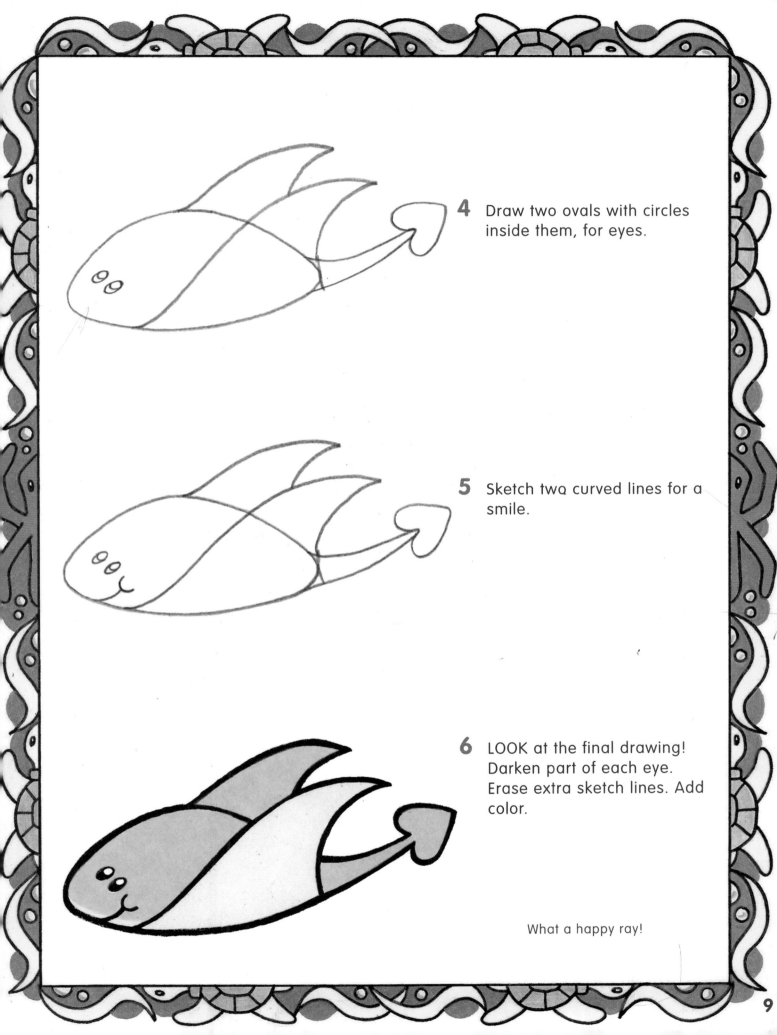

4 Draw two ovals with circles inside them, for eyes.

5 Sketch two curved lines for a smile.

6 LOOK at the final drawing! Darken part of each eye. Erase extra sketch lines. Add color.

What a happy ray!

Eel

An eel is a long snakelike fish. Let's draw a cartoon eel.

1 Sketch an oval for the head. Draw a long squiggly line to begin the body and tail.

2 Add another squiggly line, above the first line, connecting to the head and tail. Draw another connecting, squiggly line on the bottom.

3 Draw an oval, with two curved lines inside it, for the eye.

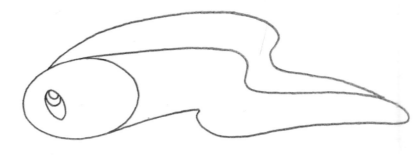

4 Draw two curved lines for a smiling mouth.

5 Add curved lines inside the eel's fin.

6 LOOK at the final drawing! Darken part of the eye. Erase extra sketch lines. Add color.

Great eel! Electric personality!

Clam

A clam is a shellfish with two hinged shells. Using simple lines and shapes, let's draw a clam.

1 Sketch an oval.

2 Add two curved lines inside the oval, for the opening of the shells.

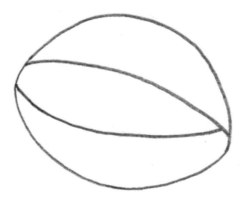

3 Draw two small curved lines on one side. Add two ovals for eyes.

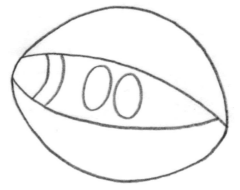

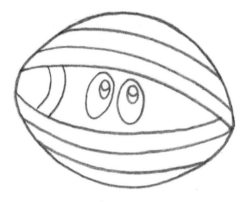

4 Add curved lines to the top and bottom of the shell. Draw an oval with a small circle inside it for each eyeball.

5 Darken part of each eyeball and the inside of the shell. Draw a shadow below the clam.

6 LOOK at the final drawing! Erase extra sketch lines. Add color and the details you see.

Happy clam!

Fish

A fish is a cold-blooded animal that lives in water. It has scales, fins and gills. Let's draw a simple cartoon fish.

1 Sketch an oval with a curved line on one side.

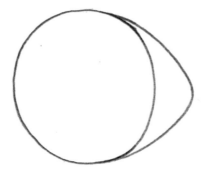

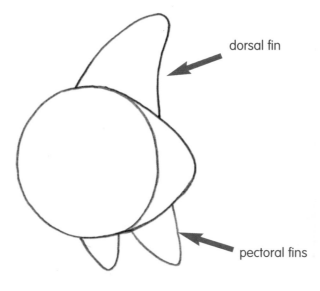

dorsal fin

pectoral fins

2 Draw a rounded wave shape for the dorsal fin. Draw curved lines for the pectoral fins.

3 Sketch a sideways valentine shape for the tail.

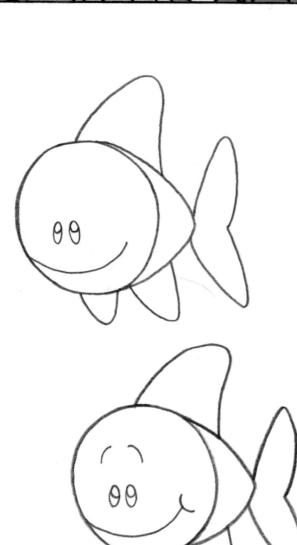

4 Draw two ovals with circles inside them, for eyes. Add a long curved line for the mouth.

5 Draw two curved lines for eyebrows. (Do real fish have eyebrows? No way! Does your cartoon fish have eyebrows—why not?) Add a tiny curved line to the side of the mouth.

6 LOOK at the final drawing! Erase extra sketch lines. Add color and details you see.

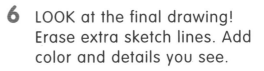

Fishy expressions

You can make a variety of expressions for your cartoon sea critters by using simple shapes and lines. Here are a few examples:

Surprised

Happy

Skeptical
("Hmmm..I'm not sure about this...")

Angry

Sad

Goofy

Sleepy

Really Happy!

Angelfish

Let's draw a cartoon angelfish.

1 Sketch an oval for the body. Draw two long curved lines to begin the tail.

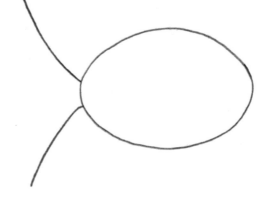

2 Sketch sharp wave shapes for the dorsal fin and pectoral fins.

3 Add two curved lines to finish the tail. Draw two curved lines for the mouth.

4 Sketch an oval for the eye. Add two curved lines inside it for the eyeball.

5 Draw two sharp wave shapes on the body. Add a curved line below the eye.

6 LOOK at the final drawing! Erase extra lines. Add color and bubbles.

Amazing angelfish!

Standing fish

Cartoon fish can stand on their tails like people stand on their feet. Let's draw one.

1 Sketch an oval for the head. Draw a rounded wave shape for the body.

2 Sketch an oval for the eye. Sketch two overlapping ovals for the tail.

3 Draw two curved lines, inside the eye oval, for the eyeball. Draw two curved lines for the mouth.

20

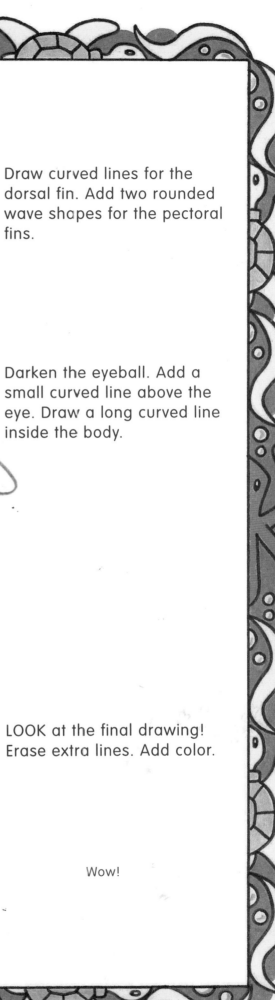

4 Draw curved lines for the dorsal fin. Add two rounded wave shapes for the pectoral fins.

5 Darken the eyeball. Add a small curved line above the eye. Draw a long curved line inside the body.

6 LOOK at the final drawing! Erase extra lines. Add color.

Wow!

Girl fish

Let's make a girl fish with long eyelashes.

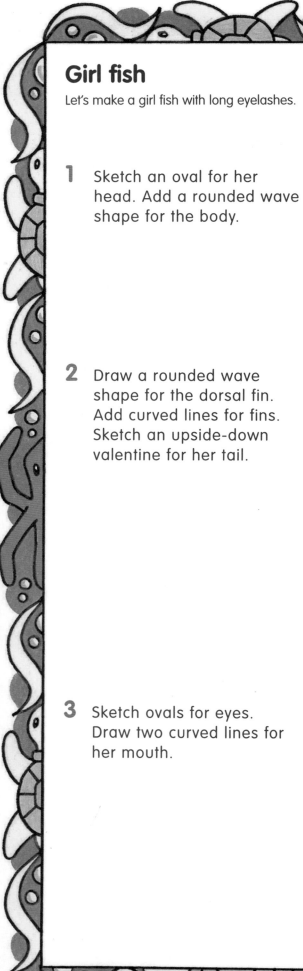

1 Sketch an oval for her head. Add a rounded wave shape for the body.

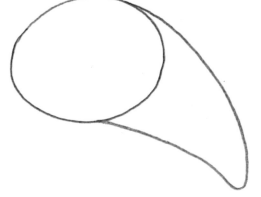

2 Draw a rounded wave shape for the dorsal fin. Add curved lines for fins. Sketch an upside-down valentine for her tail.

3 Sketch ovals for eyes. Draw two curved lines for her mouth.

4 Draw ovals for eyeballs. Darken part of each. Add curved lines below each eye.

5 Draw curved lines for eyelashes.

6 LOOK at the final drawing! Erase extra sketch lines. Add color.

Moving fish

Let's draw a fish that looks as though it's moving.

1. Sketch an oval with a rounded wave shape on one side.

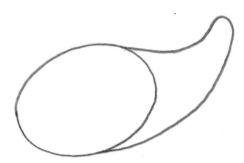

2. Add an oval with curved lines inside, for the eye. Draw two curved lines connecting to a straight line for the tail.

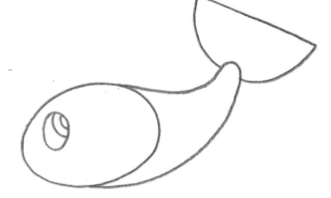

3. Sketch a sharp wave shape for the dorsal fin. Draw two curved lines for the mouth.

4 Add a small curved line below the eye. Sketch two curved lines for fins.

5 Draw curved lines inside the dorsal fin and tail.

6 LOOK at the final drawing! Erase extra lines. Add color. Draw two small curved lines on each side of the tail to make it wiggle!

Professor fish

You can add personality to your sea critters by adding clothing.

1 Sketch an oval for the head. Draw a rounded wave below it. Draw a flattened valentine shape for the tail.

2 Draw small ovals for eyes. Darken part of each. Sketch curved lines for pectoral fins.

3 Draw large circles around the eyes to begin the glasses. Add a curved line between them and one to the side. Draw curved lines for the dorsal fin.

dorsal fin

4 Draw three curved lines on top of her head, to begin a hat. Draw three curved lines for the mouth.

5 Draw a long rectangle for the top of her hat. Draw four curved lines to make the pointer.

6 LOOK at the final drawing! Erase extra lines. Add color and details.

Perfect professor! Super school!

Whale

A large sea animal that looks like a fish, the whale is actually a mammal that breathes air. Let's draw a friendly whale.

1   Sketch a large rectangle. Draw curved lines at each end for the round body.

2   Sketch an oval and two curved lines inside, for the eye. Add a curved wave shape to the other end to begin the tail.

3   Draw two curved lines for the mouth. Add two curved lines for the flippers. Sketch ovals for the tail.

4 Draw curved lines to make the spout. Draw two raindrops under the spout.

5 LOOK at the final drawing! Erase extra sketch lines. Add color.

Wow! What a whale!

Standing whale

If cartoon fish can stand up, so can cartoon whales! Let's draw one now.

1 Sketch a large oval for the head. Add two long curved lines below it for the body. Draw a flattened valentine for the tail.

2 Add an oval for the blowhole. Draw an oval with a curved line for each eye. Sketch curved lines for fins.

3 Draw two curved lines, extending from his blowhole. Draw three curved lines for the mouth.

4 Add curved lines for the top of the spout. Sketch a small curved line under his mouth for a lip.

6 LOOK at the final drawing! Erase extra lines. Add color.

Whale of a job!

Orca

The orca is a killer whale. Let's draw a friendly one.

1 Sketch a large oval for the body. Add two curved lines to the oval, to begin the tail. Draw a flattened valentine shape for the tail fins.

2 Draw a small curved line for the nose. Sketch a large rounded wave shape for the dorsal fin.

3 Draw two squashed ovals to begin the black and white pattern found on orcas. Add curved lines for flippers.

4 Sketch a small oval and curved line, inside the front oval, for the eye. Draw curved lines, extending from the flipper, to complete the orca pattern.

5 Draw curved lines for a smiling mouth.

6 LOOK at the final drawing! Erase extra lines. Add color.

Killer drawing!

Dolphin

Related to the whale, the dolphin is an intelligent water mammal with a long snout. Everybody loves dolphins! Let's draw one.

1 Make a long squashed oval shape. Add curved lines for a tail.

dorsal fin

2 Sketch a rounded wave shape for the dorsal fin. Add curved lines for flippers.

flippers

3 Draw small curved lines for the nose and chin. Sketch curved lines to begin the face shape.

4 Draw an oval and two curved lines for the eye.

5 Add a small curved line below the eye. Draw small circles for bubbles.

6 LOOK at the final drawing! Erase extra sketch lines. Add color. Notice the highlights on the back to make it look shiny.

Delightful dolphin! Nice job!

Dolphin sailor

You can give your cartoon dolphin a
little personality by adding clothing.
Let's draw a dolphin in the navy.

1 Sketch a long squashed
oval. Add curved lines
for a tail.

dorsal fin

flippers

2 Draw a rounded wave
shape for the dorsal fin.
Add curved lines for a
snout and lip. Draw
flippers.

3 Draw curved lines to
make the mouth. Add
curved lines, inside the
body, to shape the face
and front side.

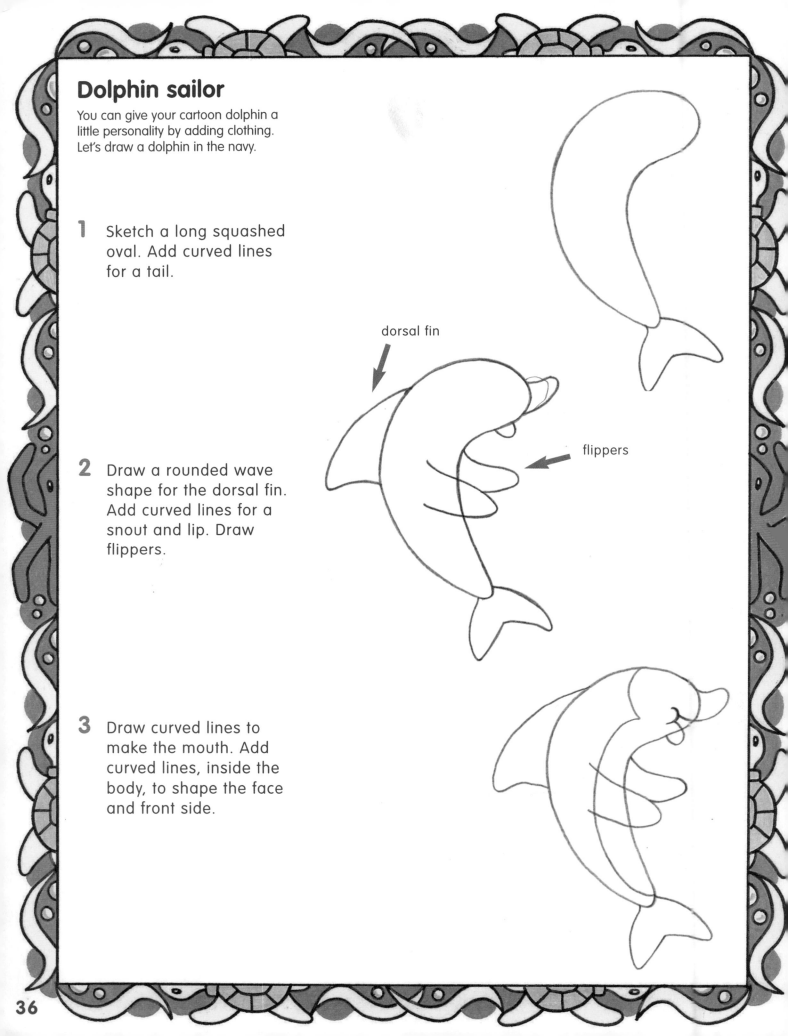

4 Draw curved lines on top of his head, to begin a sailor's cap. Sketch an oval and two curved lines for the eye.

5 Draw a small curved line on top of his cap. Add another curved line inside the cap. Sketch a small curved line below the eye.

6 LOOK at the final drawing. Erase extra sketch lines. Add color.

He's in the Navy now!

Dolphin expressions

Here are some simple shapes and lines you can use to change the facial expression of the dolphin. Try drawing each expression, and see if you can make it look real.

Tired

Skeptical

Angry

Surprised

Sad

Shocked

Nervous

Happy

Don't just LOOK at the examples.
Draw them, and you will get better
and better.

39

Dolphin action

You can also show moods and actions by changing the lines and shapes on the sea critter's body. Try sketching some of these examples to bring the dolphin to life.

Pointing

Talking

Scared

Dancing

Startled

Laughing

Glaring

Yelling

Sketch! Doodle! Play! Change your dolphin's
position slightly to make him seem more human!

Manatee

A large mammal with flippers and a flat tail, the manatee lives in warm waters and eats plants. Let's draw a cartoon manatee.

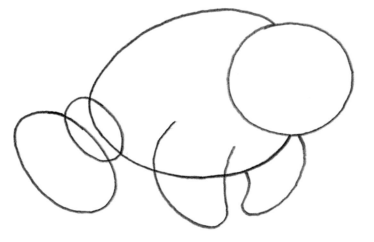

1 Sketch three overlapping ovals for the head, body and tail.

2 Add another overlapping oval for the tail. Draw two curved lines for the flippers.

3 Draw two small circles, with a curved line across each, for eyes. Sketch two curved lines to begin the nose.

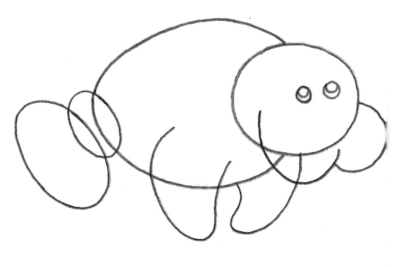

4 Darken the lower part of each eye. Add two small curved lines for nostrils.

5 Draw curved lines on his back for a small hump. Draw a small curved line on his mouth for a puffy cheek.

6 LOOK at the final drawing! Erase extra sketch lines. Add color and a few air bubbles.

Shark

A shark is a large, often fierce fish that feeds on meat. The shark has very sharp teeth. Let's draw a happy cartoon shark.

1 Sketch a long squashed oval. Add curved lines for a tail.

2 Draw a sharp wave shape for the dorsal fin. Add sharp wave shapes for the pectoral fins.

3 Draw a long curved line for the snout. Draw an oval and a curved line for the eye.

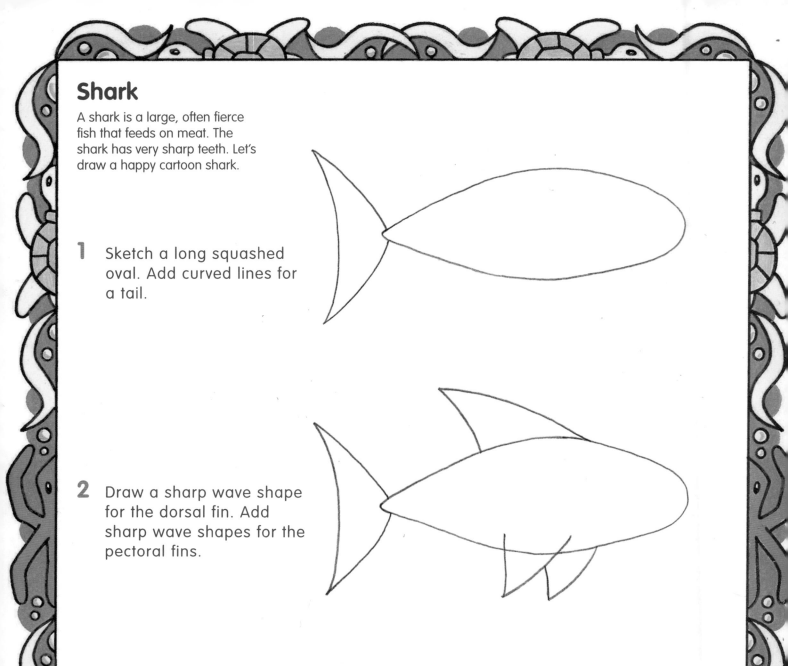

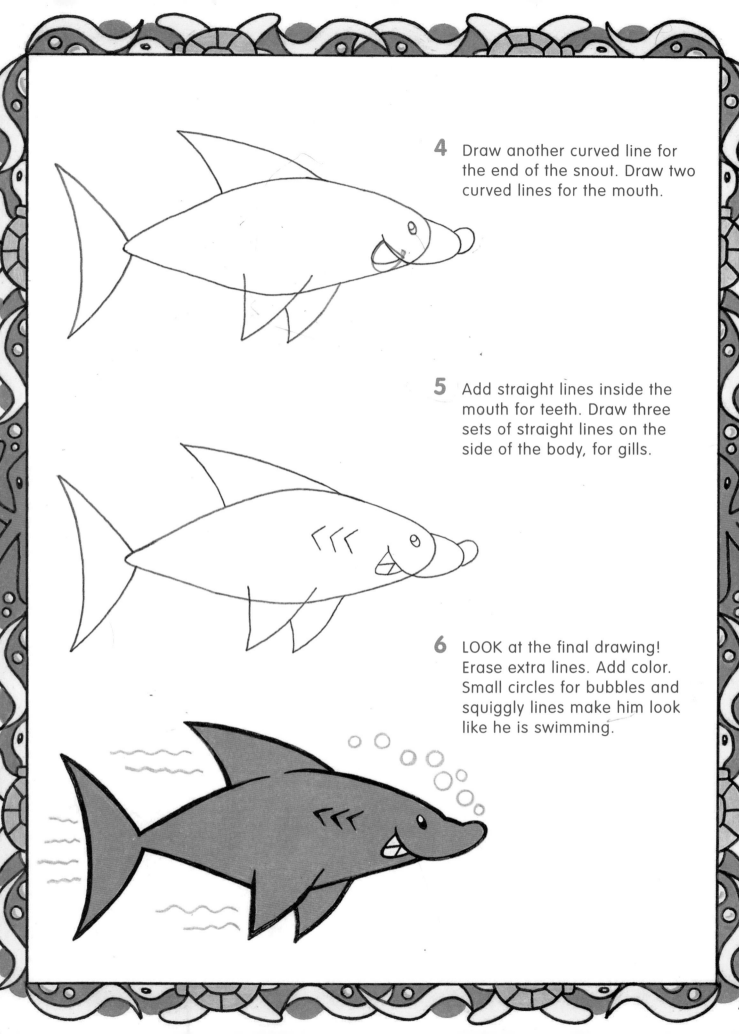

4 Draw another curved line for the end of the snout. Draw two curved lines for the mouth.

5 Add straight lines inside the mouth for teeth. Draw three sets of straight lines on the side of the body, for gills.

6 LOOK at the final drawing! Erase extra lines. Add color. Small circles for bubbles and squiggly lines make him look like he is swimming.

Standing shark

You can draw a shark standing up, too.
Let's give it a try.

1 Sketch an oval for the head. Draw a long rounded wave shape below it, for the body.

2 Draw a sharp wave shape for the dorsal fin and the pectoral fin. Draw long curved lines for the tail.

3 Sketch a curved line for the snout. Draw an oval and two curved lines for an eye. Sketch a small curved line for the chin.

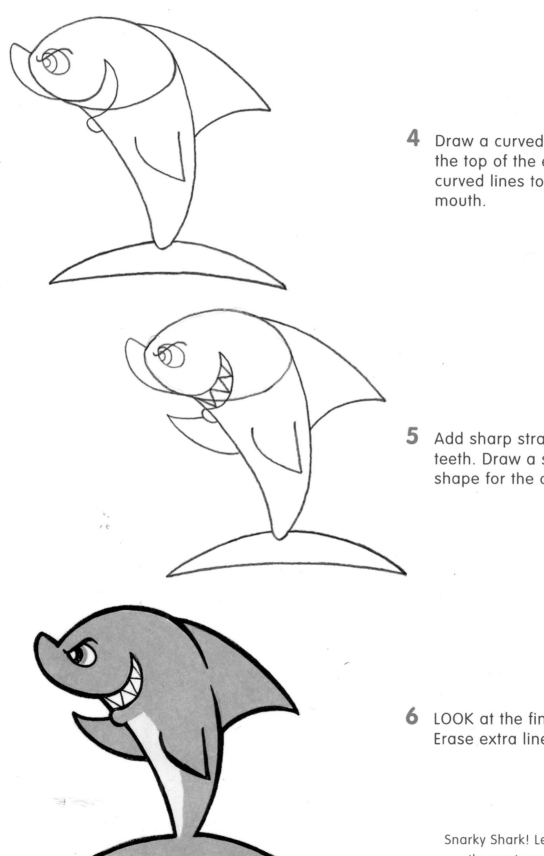

4 Draw a curved line across the top of the eye. Draw curved lines to begin the mouth.

5 Add sharp straight lines for teeth. Draw a sharp wave shape for the other fin.

6 LOOK at the final drawing! Erase extra lines. Add color.

Snarky Shark! Let's move to the next page FAST!

Octopus

A sea animal with a soft body, the octopus has eight long tentacles that it uses to catch its prey.

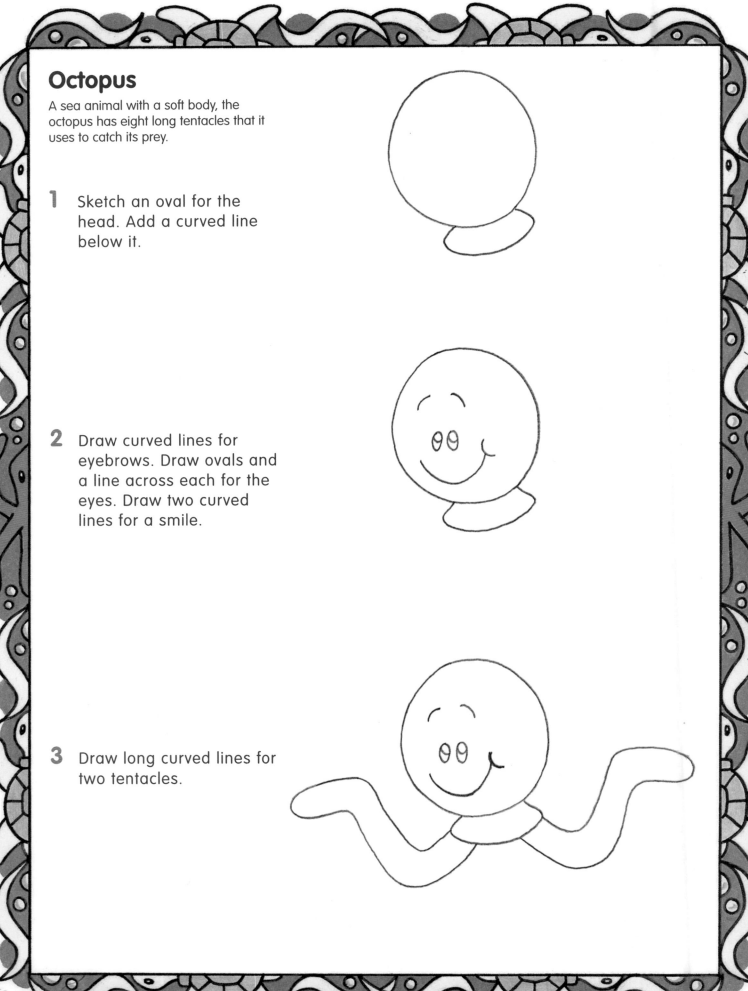

1 Sketch an oval for the head. Add a curved line below it.

2 Draw curved lines for eyebrows. Draw ovals and a line across each for the eyes. Draw two curved lines for a smile.

3 Draw long curved lines for two tentacles.

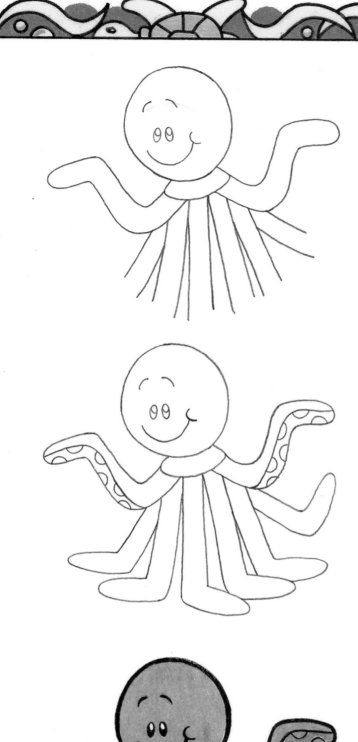

4 Sketch two long straight lines for each of the remaining six tentacles.

5 Add curved lines to the two top tentacles for suction cups. Put curved lines on the bottoms of the other tentacles.

6 LOOK at the final drawing! Erase extra lines. Add color.

Impressive octopus!

Lobster

The lobster is a sea creature with a hard shell and five pairs of legs. Let's draw a cartoon lobster with four pairs of legs.

1 Sketch a long squashed oval. Draw an upside-down valentine for a tail.

2 Draw long curved lines on the top of the squashed oval. Add two curved lines to each side.

3 Sketch large ovals on the end of the curved lines for claws. Draw two ovals and two curved line for eyes.

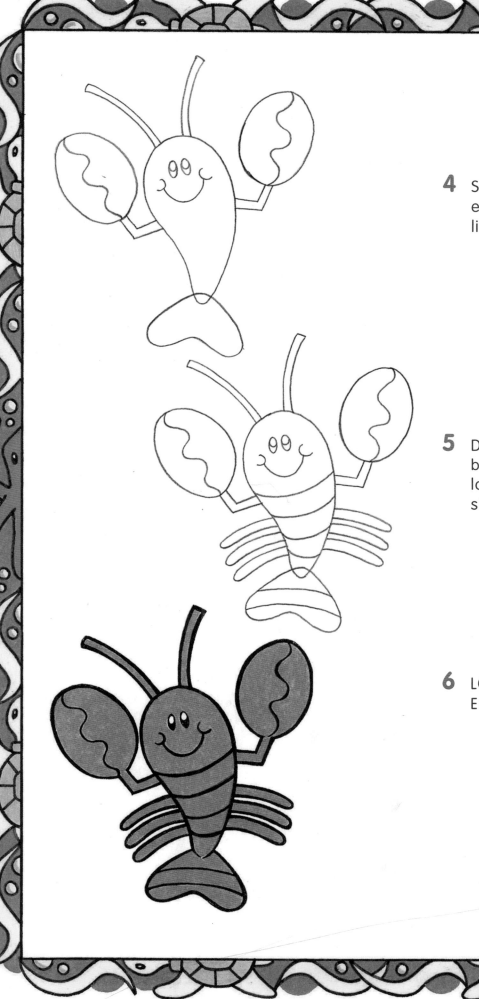

4 Sketch squiggly lines inside each claw. Add three curved lines for a mouth.

5 Draw curved lines inside the body and tail. Sketch three long curved lines on each side of the body for legs.

6 LOOK at the final drawing! Erase extra lines. Add color.

Lovely lobster!

Crab

The crab is a water creature with a hard shell, eight legs, and two claws, or pinchers. Let's draw a cartoon crab!

1   Sketch a large oval for the head. Add two smaller ovals for eyes.

2   On each side, draw curved lines with a small oval on the end to begin two legs. Draw eyeballs inside the eyes.

3   Sketch a larger oval on top of the arms. Add curved lines for the pinchers.

4 Draw three curved line for a smiling mouth.

5 Draw long curved lines for six legs. Add small curved lines in the middle of each leg for joints.

6 LOOK at the final drawing! Erase extra lines. Add color.

Not a very crabby crab!

Seahorse

The seahorse is a small ocean fish with a head shaped like that of a horse and a long curving tail. Let's draw a cartoon seahorse.

1 Sketch an oval for the head. Sketch a tilted oval for the body. Draw two curved lines connecting the ovals.

2 Draw an oval with a line across it for the eye. Draw two long winding curved lines for the tail.

3 Look at the snout. Draw curved lines with an oval at the end for the snout. Draw curved lines for fins on the head and back.

4 Add curved lines to make the mouth and chin. Draw a long curved line along the neck and body.

5 Add curved lines to the fins, chest and neck. Draw curved lines for a side fin.

6 LOOK at the final drawing! Erase extra lines. Add color.

A fun one to horse around with!

Sea monster

In cartoons, you can even bring legendary creatures to life! Let's draw a sea monster.

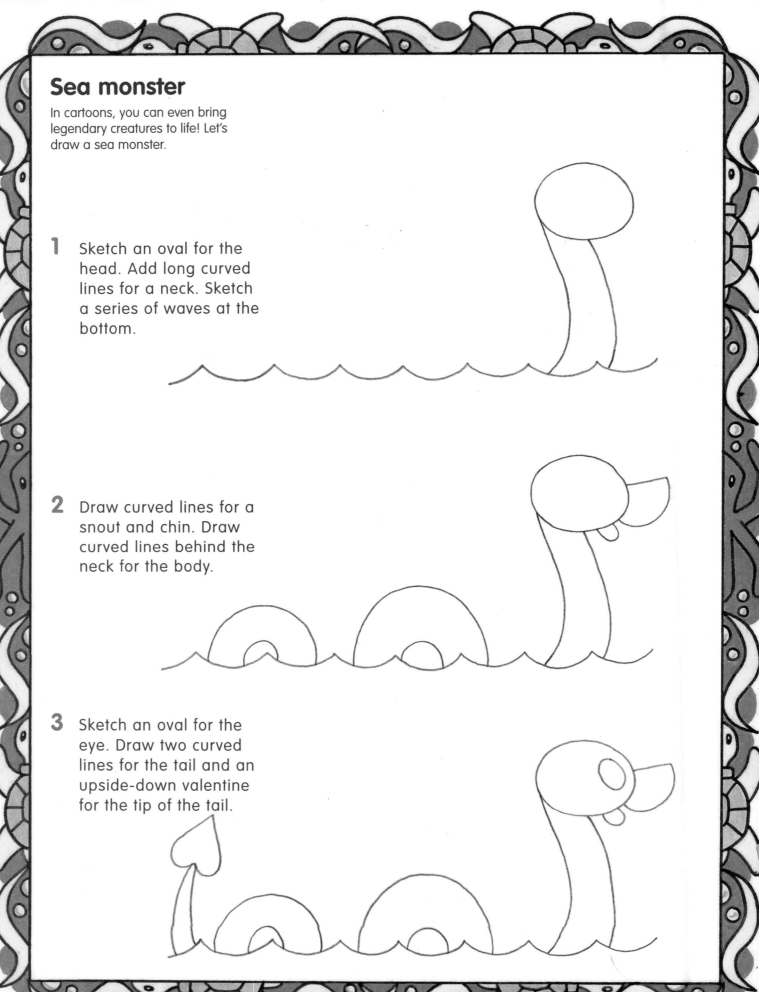

1   Sketch an oval for the head. Add long curved lines for a neck. Sketch a series of waves at the bottom.

2   Draw curved lines for a snout and chin. Draw curved lines behind the neck for the body.

3   Sketch an oval for the eye. Draw two curved lines for the tail and an upside-down valentine for the tip of the tail.

4 Draw a curved line on top of the head. Draw an oval and curved lines for the eye. Add a small curved line for a nostril. Add a long curved line along the neck.

5 Draw a series of sharp, jagged wave shapes along the neck and back. Add small curved lines along the inside of the neck.

6 LOOK at the final drawing! Erase extra lines. Add color.

Sea background

You have drawn some great cartoon sea critters. Now, let's draw some interesting surroundings for them to live in.

1   Sketch curved lines to make rocks.

2   Add small lines and dots to give them texture.

3   Sketch long curved lines to make seaweed.

4   Draw small ovals for pebbles and little dots for sand.

5 Add curved lines behind the rocks to form the seabed. Add little curved lines around the rocks. Draw a rounded star shape for a starfish.

6 LOOK at the final drawing! Erase extra lines. Add color and draw your favorite cartoon sea critters in the scene.

Congratulations! You've created a SUPER sea world.

Keep going

You have drawn some extraordinary cartoon sea critters. Now, use what you have learned in this book to add some clothing to them. Use your imagination to give each critter more personality.

Award yourself! On the next page you'll find an award certificate you can photocopy to let the world know you're a **Cartoonist's Apprentice First Class!**

Have you enjoyed this book? Find out about other books in this series and see sample pages online at

www.123draw.com